Baseball's MVPs

READING POWER

JUSTIN MORNEAU

Joe Gaspar

PowerKiDS press.
New York

For David and Christine Power, two proud Minnesotans

Published in 2011 by The Rosen Publishing Group, Inc.
29 East 21st Street, New York, NY 10010

First Edition

Editor: Amelie von Zumbusch
Book Design: Kate Laczynski
Photo Researcher: Jessica Gerweck

Photo Credits: Cover, p. 1 Brad Mangin/MLB Photos via Getty Images; p. 4 Paul Jasienski/Getty Images; p. 7 J. Meric/Getty Images; p. 8 Bruce Kluckhohn/Getty Images; pp. 11, 20 Bruce Kluckhohn/MLB Photos via Getty Images; p. 12 John Grieshop/MLB Photos via Getty Images; p. 15 Dave Kaup/Getty Images; p. 16 Lisa Blumenfeld/Getty Images; p. 19 Kevork Djansezian/Getty Images; p. 22 Tom Dahlin/Getty Images.

Library of Congress Cataloging-in-Publication Data

Gaspar, Joe.
Justin Morneau / Joe Gaspar.
p. cm. — (Baseball's mvps)
Includes index.
ISBN 978-1-4488-0633-1 (library binding) —
ISBN 978-1-4488-1790-0 (pbk.) — ISBN 978-1-4488-1791-7 (6-pack)
1. Morneau, Justin—Juvenile literature. 2. Baseball players—United States—Biography—Juvenile literature. I. Title.
GV865.M644G37 2011
796.3570972—dc22
[B] 2009051147

Manufactured in the United States of America

CPSIA Compliance Information: Batch #WS10PK: For Further Information contact Rosen Publishing, New York, New York at 1-800-237-9932

CONTENTS

This is Justin Morneau.
He is a baseball player.

Morneau is from Canada. He was born in New Westminster, British Columbia.

CANADA
33

Cub
Twins

For a while, Morneau played both **hockey** and baseball. In the end, he picked baseball.

Justin Morneau plays for the Minnesota Twins.

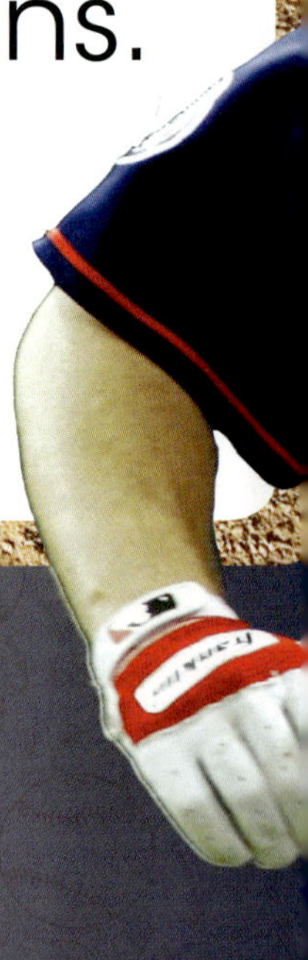

Twins
33

Morneau played his first game with the Twins in 2003.

Morneau plays first base. He is one of the team's biggest stars.

MINNESOTA

MORNEAU
33
MINNESO

Other Twins players like playing with Morneau. He helps his team win.

Morneau is a strong hitter. He has hit many **home runs**.

MORNEAU
33

KENESAW MOUNTAIN LANDIS
MEMORIAL BASEBALL AWARD
MOST
VALUABLE PLAYER
AMERICAN LEAGUE
Twins
33
125
Louisville
Slugger

In 2006, he was named the American **League** MVP, or most **valuable** player.

Morneau is one of today's best baseball players.

BOOKS

Here are more books to read about Justin Morneau and baseball:

Frisch, Aaron. *Minnesota Twins*. World Series Champions. Mankato, MN: The Creative Company, 2009.

Stewart, Mark. *The Minnesota Twins*. Team Spirit. Chicago: Norwood House Press, 2008.

WEB SITES

Due to the changing nature of Internet links, PowerKids Press has developed an online list of Web sites related to the subject of this book. This site is updated regularly. Please use this link to access the list:
www.powerkidslinks.com/bmvp/jm/

GLOSSARY

hockey (HO-kee) A sport played by two teams on ice.

home runs (HOME RUNZ) Hits in which the batter touches all the bases and scores a run.

league (LEEG) A group of sports teams.

valuable (VAL-yoo-bul) Important.

INDEX